Vladimír Holan

DOLOUR

Vladimír Holan

DOLOUR

Verses from years 1949–1955

© Vladimír Holan estate, c/o Aura-pont, 2010
© Translation from Czech: Josef Tomáš, 2010
   Edited by Betty Boyd
© Illustrations: Jáchym Šerých, 2010
© Foreword: Jiří Brabec, 2010

Originally published by Československý spisovatel, Praha, 1966, under the title *Bolest*

All rights reserved

This book is copyright. Subject to statutory exception and to provisions of relevant collective licensing agreements, no part of this publication may be reproduced, stored in a retrieval system, or transmitted in any form, or by any means, without the prior written permission of the author's estate.

Printed and bound in the United Kingdom

Typeset in Regent and Aichel

This book is sold subject to the condition that it shall not, by way of trade or otherwise, be lent, re-sold, hired out or otherwise circulated without the publisher's prior consent in any form of binding or cover other than that which it is published and without a similar condition including this condition being imposed on the subsequent purchaser.

ISBN 978-1-84549-473-5

Published 2010 by arima publishing
ASK House, Northgate Avenue
Bury St Edmunds, Suffolk IP32 6BB
t: (+44)01284 700321
www.arimapublishing.com

Czech poets in arima publishing

Vladimír Holan
The First Testament, 2005
Soliloquy with Shakespeare, 2007
Narrative Poems I, 2008
Narrative Poems II, 2010

Jiří Orten
Selected Poems, 2007

Josef Tomáš
The World in My Mouth, 2009

The translation of this book has been kindly subsidized
by the Ministry of Culture of the Czech Republic

Contents

Introduction	17
At Mother's, After Many Years Away	29
Even Though	30
Eva	31
A Rendezvous	32
A Cave of Words	33
But Time...	34
A Triangle	35
There Is	36
Dawn	38
An Accident	40
Before New Year's Eve	41
Audacity	42
A Poet	43
It Is Not	44
During Insomnia	45
In a Cruel Year	46
At Daybreak	47
To the Daughter of P.B.	48
A Tear	49
Europe	50
An Encounter in an Elevator	51
Deep in the Night	52
Early Spring	53
At Harvest Time	54
A House	55

One Morning	56
Lot Fornicates with His Daughters	57
And Again	58
Autumn I	59
Recollection I	60
The Snow	61
A Test I	62
Daybreak I	64
How?	65
Yet Again	66
What Might She Be Reading?	67
When It Rains on Sunday	68
A Dying Poet	69
The Noonday Witch	70
After St Martin's I	71
Any Night, Especially The One Before Dawn	72
There Are	73
She	74
Without a Title I	75
Yes?	76
Each of Them	77
Grief	78
The Pedal Curve of a Parabola	79
She – Even the Sun Sometimes Replicates Itself and Points to Where It Is Not	80
Autumn in Všenory	81
When Observing the Sun Spot at a Hornbeam	82
Beauty Without Joy	83
The Distant One...	84
Verses	85
A Resort	86

All the Time	87
Daybreak II	88
A Stopover of a Courier	89
The Sun at Candlemas	90
At Insomnia	91
Those Others	92
Let the Dead Bury the Dead	93
To Whom?	94
A Judgement	95
After the Death of My Sister Rose	96
The Adder Hunter	97
Is this Enough?	98
Dies Caniculares 1951	99
Recollection II	100
Non Cum Platone	102
The Eyes of a Man	103
Only Over the Wall of a Boneyard	104
Autumn II	105
After St Martin's II	106
In Temptation	107
Mountains Go, Flowers Go	108
Under the Hill of Blaník	109
Near the River Jizera	110
An October Day	111
During a Night	112
Ubi Nullus Ordo, Sed Perpetuus Horror	113
At Marat's Grave	114
An Old Priest	115
Down to the Last Cent	116
Spices of the Holy Ghost	117
You Found...	118

A Watchman's Song	119
The Asphalt Princess	120
Home	121
They Have...	122
Without a Title II	123
A Fall	124
A Test II	125
The Body of a Woman	126
You Know It, My God !	127
The Fourth Month	128
† To My Sister Rose	129
What Then?	130
December in a Village	131
Resurrection	132
A Voice	133
Deep in the Night	134
October I	135
Premonition	136
Poesy	137
But Love Both...	138
A Pine	139
In a Cloud	140
Without a Title III	141
A Test III	142
A Chicken	143
A Night	144
Quite Certainly	145
Death	146
In the Nothingness	147
On a Biting Night	148
I Don't Understand	149

El Todo	150
Once	151
The Blinded Ones	152
Inside You	153
Seen from an Express Train	154
A Test IV	155
Children	156
In Between	157
In September, Close to 2 am	158
Mors Ascendit Per Fenetras	159
Nothing Melancholy	160
Maliciously	161
Lovers	162
Never Enough Tears	163
When It Is Foggy, Rust Falls upon Old and Beauty Falls upon Young Virgins	164
An Oak Tree	165
The Year 1953	166
Partus Labyrinthis	167
Who?	168
At Harvest Time	169
Remembrance of September 1952	170
At the End of June	171
Why?	172
A Sunspot	173
A Dream	174
La Belle Dame Sans Merci	175
Autumn III	176
Blackness	177
During Illness	178

The Epoch	179
A Virgin	180
At Night	181
At a Fountain with the Ruby Fairy	182
To Rose	183
Sultry Heat I	184
Dust	185
Not Before	186
An Autumn Night	187
October II	188
On Spy Wednesday	189
Along the Way	190
Towards Poesy	191
Awoken...	192
Sultry Heat II	193
Someone	194
Adonis	195
After a Storm	196
They Paint	197
In Fallow	198
Succinctly	199
On the Sixth of January	200
It Was Already Late	201
You May Ask	202
A Sparrow	203
Goodbye	204
But	205

Introduction
by Dr Jiří Brabec

Why so rough is your flight
and why does it stall?
– Fifteen years, day and night,
I talked to a wall,

and it's this wall I drag
out from my hell
to let it be the tag
on what is to tell.

(*A Wall*, 21ˢᵗ June 1963)

Few European poets experienced the catastrophic era of war and totalitarian regimes with such intensity as Vladimír Holan. He was often characterised as a "poet of apocalypse" but it would be more fitting to call him a poet of an endangered human being, a poet of the drama of a world in which human values had totally disintegrated.

He experimented with prose (for example in the set of texts *Lemuria*, from the Forties) and was discovering a new form of poetic epics (for example in the collection

Narrative Poems, which he wrote in the Fifties), but lyric poetry remained his sphere of constant exploration of the mystery of being, the elusive meaning of the human sojourn in the world. The poetry collections of the Thirties – *Breezing*; *Arch*; *Stone, You are Coming* – are wholly given up to the search for an autonomous form..."Put symbols behind things" was Holan's creed at that time.

Yet, during the war, he challenged this yearning for artistic "perfection and consistency", an aspiration so characteristic of modern poetry, for example the work of Rainer Maria Rilke or Paul Valéry. "I too once used magic formulae to conjure..." Holan wrote in the fragments *Rags, Bones, Skins*, published in 1946. "But today I understand that it can be a worn step, a mother's ring or grave that tears you away from games with language and towards the tragic speech of some little valley... Versus-verse also means versus-against! With poetry it is the same as with the wild plant *moonwort [Botrichium lunaris]*, known as the *opening* plant. This plant, endowed with magic powers to discover the miraculous, experiences nothing but obstacles in its path. While (as common people believe) all plants float with the current, the *moonwort* floats against the current..." However, this turn to the real world did not mean that Holan was prepared to become submissive to the topics of the day.

Holan's lyric is the realm of creative freedom, the construction of space for "cruel questioning". This is clear in the diptych *Without Title* and *Advancing* (Holan later combined them in the volume *But There is Still Music*) of 1939 to

1948. The poems waver between faith in the liberation of humanity and a persistent scepticism – "Are we in dissolution or are we holding on?" Themes of the finite and infinite, the universal and unique, of "spectres" and "reality" keep returning. Once the master of original metaphors, Holan becomes more restrained and less grandiose in his language. Free verse form appears, allowing relaxed narrative and reflection to address the reader directly. But Holan's work remains distinctive for its unexpected shifts of meaning, temporal jumps, abrupt changes of theme, the inter-penetration of the figurative and non-figurative levels...

The collection *Dolour* has a key position in Holan's work. The poems were written in the years 1948–1955, when he was also writing the poetic cycle *Fear*. To the words *dolour* and *fear*, we need to add a third: *walls*, which, at the time, became the theme of several poems. These three words; dolour, fear and walls, refer to the tragedy of Holan's personal life, but above all to the history of the time. In February 1948 a Communist putsch finally converted Czechoslovakia to a satellite of the Soviet Union. Holan had been a member of the Communist Party until 1945, but he radically rejected the dictatorship of the Party. He voluntarily retreated into solitude and, for the rest of his life, hardly ever left his flat on the island of Kampa in Prague. He was completely irreconcilable to the ruling regime. He judged some of his own post-war poems extremely harshly, although they had been an expression of joy at the end of the war and were, in no fundamental way, disfigured by the rhetoric of the time.

"Hope in man – even the most enthusiastic one –
flung me, in the end
under a power all too human
and, thus, without God ... Hence, I have to exist
and I am already punished,
especially because I may have led other souls astray..."

Under the totalitarian regime, even poetry had its prescribed role: the present and the future had to be glorified as the culmination of the historical process . Optimism, praise of the regime and odes to its leaders were essential attributes of socialist poetry. One of the most important Czech poets of the 20th century, Vítězslav Nezval, the former surrealist, wrote several poems (for example *Stalin* and *The Song of Peace*, which fully met the stipulated requirements of the Communist regime. It was precisely these ideological directives – which had to be fulfilled, if a poet was to be published at all – that were entirely unacceptable to Holan. The exultant euphoria of a cruel world formed the background of *Dolour* and *Fear*, as well as the *Walls* that surrounded him. Holan bears witness to a time of disillusion, disbelief, hypocrisy and crime. Only in a very few verses does he directly express his contempt for the "enemies".

"But I have had enough of your insolence
which permeates everything
where it wished to comprehend
but could not embrace...
But a calamity is coming,
of which you could never even have dreamt..."

Direct polemic is very rare in Holan's *Dolour*. What is distinctive is the scenery of the poems – the season of autumn and winter often returns, the time of night and dawn (*Autumn in Všenory, October Day, December in the Village, On a Biting Night, Sleeplessness*). Questions showing a recurrent search for the meaning of events appear in the titles of the poems – *Yes? How? To Whom?* and *Why?*. All the pain is spread out in reflective poems, where the everyday and the transcendent blend together; where commentary on particular experiences, memories, evoked scenes and paradoxical encounters, ambiguous confrontations and ordinary events take on the contours of a timeless message. Yet the poet's solitude ("It is terrible to live, for it is necessary to stay / in the appalling reality of these years...") is abundantly stocked up with people. His poems are a latent dialogue, where there is always someone to whom the poem is addressed or who is making an actual appearance in it. In the reflection, evoked by a concrete event, these others form a fictional community that allows Holan to carry on a continual conversation. Solitude, enlivened by miniature stories, saves reflective thought from monotony; the small space defined by his four *walls* is charged with dramatic action.

Holan's lifelong struggle to find a new form – a poetry that would avoid all improvising, period schematics, stereotypical symbolism, poetic clichés ("Poetics merely destroys poetry"), continues in *Dolour*:

"I always looked for a word
that had been spoken only once,
even for a word that had never yet been uttered.
I should have looked for ordinary words".

This discovery of simplicity, the everyday as a window on the mystery of life, is closely bound up in *Dolour* with the day to day experience of his voluntary personal exclusion from ordinary life. Nevertheless, the loss of all external support enabled human beings to manifest themselves in authentic forms in his poetry.

"You are alone. Minimize your gestures as much as possible, because there is nothing to admire!" says Holan, and it is precisely this cohesiveness – the closest possible link between the poetry and the concrete human destiny – that gives *Dolour* its unique power and sets it among the supreme achievements of 20th century European poetry.

Translator's note: On May 17, 2010 Dr Jiri Brabec received the most prestigious Czech F.X. Šalda Prize for literary criticism.

In memory of

JOSEF ČAPEK,
JOSEF HORA
AND
FRANTIŠEK HALAS

*The closer to harmony,
the harder the dissonances become.*

J. S. Bach

At Mother's, After Many Years Away

This is the moment when the fire in the hearth
needs to be banked up with ash...
The hands of your old mother will do it;
the hands that tremble, but the hands
whose trembling is still a measure
of reassurance... Dandled by them, you fall asleep
and feel good... Custom, warmth, delight and quietude,
and breath's intimacy with something almost blissfully
    sensual
are both received and given,
when you lose yourself in yourself:
they negate that you are over forty.
And really, if, close to morning, you sob out aloud,
then it is only because
a child never laughs while dreaming
but always only cries... A child!

Even Though

Even though, my love, you are always eluding me,
you are my ever-present presence; oh, for certain!
Like a waterfall:
even though the water – always the same – always leaves it,
the fall always stays in the same place...

Eva

To Marie Tomášová

It was in new wine... Autumn
was already entwining bottles with a split wicker,
and the snake – no longer on the stone but under the
 heather –
lay down on its belly and covered itself with its little
 backbone.

"Beauty destroys love; love destroys beauty!" she told me.
And, as we once used to sacrifice
to the local antique goddesses in odd numbers,
at the same time she was thinking only about herself,
carelessly envisaging
eternity without immortality...

She was so beautiful that if someone asked me
which way I walked with her, surely I would not talk
about the land (far from it, because I felt such a
 helplessness
of words within me that only rain falling on a prison
could spell my silence).
She was so beautiful that I wanted
to live again, but in a completely different way.
She was so beautiful that the whole of my madness
was still waiting for the folly of my passion...

A Rendezvous

Rain without trees... Some sodden hay...
Turning on the gas... A cloud, fried on the pan of the
    moon...
Some twinkling... Some blinking... Some disappearance of
    shapes...
They nearly tripped over a wheelbarrow full of clay from
    the graveyard...
"Are you fond of me?" – Yes!
"Do you love me?" – No!

A Cave of Words

With impunity, a youth enters the cave of words
with a light... Fearless, he hardly surmises where he finds
    himself... Young, even if suffering,
he does not know what pain can be... Prematurely
    masterful,
he runs away, without stepping in, and blames
the century for not having reached its full age...

A cave of words!...
Only a real poet – and that at his own risk –
loses his wings because of madness, as well as
how to return them to Earth's heaviness
without harming the one who attracts Earth...

A cave of words! Only a real poet
returns – already old – from its silence
to find a crying child,
abandoned by the world at its threshold...

But Time...

"What's in your heart?" my life asked me.
The question came so suddenly
and so truthfully
that I wanted to say: Nothing!

But Time (when standing close to a stone pillar,
once forced entire temples to come down)
said to me: "You liar! The place
that women congested for you
is still vacant, but only in Hell!"

A Triangle

When a virgin lies down on her side,
she unwittingly overturns the whole grove.

When she lies down on her stomach,
she forgets herself because of her desire for all the roots.

And when she lies down on her back,
she knows that someone has already erected his maypole
straight into the chimney.

This someone, by then in front of a pint jug,
bites his lips and, at his pencil's whim,
writes it down... Perhaps, I daresay,
he then seals up the envelope
because he is ashamed of his letter.

There Is

There is such fate
that what's in it without a quiver is not firm.

There is such love
that you fall short of the world, be it only for a little step.

There is such delight
that you punish the arts when the arts are sinful.

There is such silence
that female mouths look as if shame was only a matter of
    sex.

There is such hair, forged by a falling star,
that it is the devil who is parting it.

There is such solitude
that you look only at salt, and only with one eye.

There is such coldness
that you suffocate the doves to warm your wings with them.

There is such heaviness
that, among those who are falling, you have already fallen.

And there is such tranquillity
that you must voice it: and namely you, *rightly* you!

Dawn

It is the moment when a priest goes along the devil's back
to celebrate Mass.

It is the moment when the heavy suitcase of dawn
regards our spine as a zip-fastener.

It is the moment when it's freezing and the sun doesn't
    shine,
but the gravestone is still warm
because it's moving.

It is the moment when the lake freezes up from its banks,
but man from his heart.

It is the moment when dreams are more
than a flea-bite into Marsyas' skin.

It is the moment when trees, injured by a doe,
wait for her to lick off the wounds.

It is the moment when the vulva of a horologe
collects the splinters of hourly words.

It is the moment when only someone's love
dares to descend to the stalactitic cave of those tears
that were secretly suppressed, yet worked secretly.

It is the moment when you must write a poem
and say it differently, quite differently...

An Accident

In the fog, and as if it dwelled there,
there is a pinewood.
And more uncovered, and thus much closer
and somehow put in danger, there is a beech grove.
Overhead, above the forest and the grove,
there are clouds without birds.
Underneath, across a jealous meadow,
a winged man wobbles...
Two wrongs do make a right.

Before New Year's Eve

What may this nocturnal wind bring?
Will it be rain, snow or a letter?
A letter from whom? A good letter or a bad one?

Everything, even that which is most withdrawn,
is still concealing something,
but, in the end, jealousy will reveal everything –
even that which can't be communicated...

Audacity

In Memory of Jakub Deml

For a long time now, you aspired to write a poem
that would be so simple and so pellucid it would be
    invisible,
annoying no one here, but, perhaps, being read
by an angel!... And you contemplated frequently
what such a poem should sing about,
even if you felt that it could be about anything,
yet written in such a simple and transparent way
that it had to be invisible...

A Poet

Being endowed, you used to feel your mission.
If only – in it – you were the one who gave!
However, if you imagined that your verses
acted on other souls destructively
(and they could have acted that way,
because even decency could still be proud),
then woe is you!

It Is Not

Where we are at this moment is not indifferent.
Some stars are coming perilously close
to each other. And, also here below,
a forcible separation of lovers happens
simply for speeding up time
by the pulsation of their hearts.

Only simple people don't look for happiness...

During Insomnia

I was alone, absolutely alone;
even a night's sleep left me...
Suddenly, I heard, not words perhaps but sounds,
and the sounds were always no longer than three sighs,
like wind and flour...
"What could it be? I have no time to wait!"
I whispered and, having scooped up my hair with wine,
I stood up and groped about nakedly.
A little while later, the black warmth of my hand
opened a wardrobe... The moths
were moving the garments there...

I am more mortal than my body...

In a Cruel Year

"How not to be?" a friend asked me today.
"How not to be and not to cause any harm
to one's mother, wife or child?"

Star-gazers say that it was *a catastrophe*
that brought our planet into existence.
Life on Earth is really atrocious.
It is the devil who divides,
then puts together
our worldly hope for this world...

After all, even the cross of Christ the Lord
was, in fact, a gallows...

At Daybreak

Yes, it already dawns... It is like dirty underwear
on the bathed body of a beautiful women...
To touch, oh, only to touch!
But nothing remains, not even a dream.
Aloft at the top, you too plough the sands,
because whoever descends into poesy
won't step up any more...

To the Daughter of P.B.

As soon as you appeared, you gave already!
Why then don't you want to be who you are?
Why do you want to agonize yourself over poesy
just to be here for a little longer than you are going to be?

A Tear

There is no single human tear
that would not, at the same time, stream
down the face of the Virgin Mary.

There is no single human tear
that would not, at the same time, be shed
by the Guardian Angel.

But there is no single human tear
that you could, at the same time, discover
in the eyes of a snake...

Europe

All dungeons of the world are built with the stones
that were showered on Jesus.

And pecuniary hands continue doing it,
so that *they can't* give even a pittance.

Farther then grows dungeon upon dungeon,
and almost all of us are already imprisoned inside them,

and we wear away in them, as if our very God wishes
not to be inside us until He is without us...

An Encounter in an Elevator

We stepped into the elevator and were there, two of us,
	alone.
We looked at each other and did nothing else.
Two lives, a moment, fullness, bliss...
At the fifth floor, she stepped out and I, who continued,
realized that I would never see her again,
that it was an encounter once and for all,
that if I followed her, I would follow her like a dead man,
and that, even if she returned to me,
her return would be only from another world.

Deep in the Night

To Jaroslav Seifert

"How not to be!" you ask, and you even pronounce it...
Take a tree or a stone: they remain silent,
though both come from a word and, thus, are mute,
as long as the word is horrified by what became of it...
But *names*, they still have them. The names: a pine-tree,
a maple, an aspen... And other names: feldspar,
basalt, clinkstone, love... Beautiful names,
except that they are horrified by what became of them...

Early Spring

The light is in the lower state of clouds.
Snow already creeps down.
The air combs its hair on the willows.
The earth is retrospecting. The fountains are surmising.
For the love of life, even a crow
flies past without any sound,
and a seed too is lacking words...

But not all that's silent is mute.
The cave at the left hand's knoll is very calm.
And if it soon fills up with soldiers,
it will be because of some chatterer.
Homer, in front of the vulva of a Trojan mare in foal...

At Harvest Time

When I saw you kneeling at a sheaf in today's heat-stroke
and pulling the binder into a knot,
you, the golden one upon the gold –
apparently in love with the boy over there,
who, every now and then, turned around after you –
I had to think about the one I love
and who does not love me;
about the one who, night after night, rests:
the white one in white, and needs
not even herself...

She, one out of thousandfold spectators
at executions...

A House

It's not an eye-catching house, even if a little fat:
the way the sparrows cut it out of lean greenery...
It does not frustrate its neighbourhood, and, likewise,
one of its open windows is just inhaling and exhaling,
and its door too is truly just an entrance.
You would say: splendour and peace and quietude and life...

And yet, inside it, there lives someone
who killed a man in order to save a woman,
but also someone who, in order to save himself,
started killing men and women...

One Morning

One morning, as you opened the door,
you found little dancing shoes on the doorstep.
They were so kissable, and you kissed them right away,
and, after many years, you felt joy once more;
all your tears, suppressed a long time ago,
were rising up to your smile,
and you smiled then and sang soulfully
in that young silence...
And you did not ask who was that beauty
who placed those shoes there, on the doorstep.
And you never learned it,
but you still re-live
that blissful moment many times...

Lot Fornicates with His Daughters

As early as when fleeing from Sodom, bursting through the
 egg gate,
they felt: the father a stream, and his daughters their
 deltas...
After an hour of flight Lot stopped and turned back:
the city behind him (even if still ringing its big alarm bell)
was now nothing more but scorched fire and drowned
 water...

There was truly no reason to exchange shoeless horses for
 donkeys,
and so they stayed in the nearest cave to inhale and exhale.
Later, they lit a fire and talked...
And, while he didn't comprehend
that there is space even between the eyes,
right in front of him those two were clasping
the drunken wine of their wombs in such a way
that he uncorked them with his fifth thumb...

Even the sin of a saint can be a prophecy.

And Again

Each time, when Cleopatra was to cross a wasteland,
she ordered male pylons to be erected there.
As she passed through meadows,
she invoked Hekete, the goddess-frog,
who protected women in childbirth.
However, when she navigated a river,
titillated by her nipples into the memory of her thighs,
she understood that a ship made of pictures
was not a figurative ship.

Only poetics destroys poetry...

Autumn I

Hunters, who suddenly stumble upon lovers,
would be blinded by their excessive proximity.
Also, to kill a snake would be a sin,
because one can't see a dead woman.
Although the air looks down at the colours,
the least yellow is the yellowness itself.

Intimate pellucidity. Square-shouldered forgetfulness.
A cube, filled up with the memory of a sphere.
Who would not feel languor for a ruin?

Recollection I

The sun was setting, falling upon a dung heap,
like an office lamp
that, before being switched off, still illuminates
a deplorable locust-tree in the street...
A girl stood at the fountain of a little town.
She was beautiful. I started a conversation with her.
She seemed to be almost grateful: each of my words
was an inducement for her not to be of this earth.
She knew nothing about nakedness:
that it could actually be dressed up in such a way
that only her dress uncovered it.
She laughed; she played with her ringlet and coughed a
    little.
And her commonness was so mysterious that it no longer
    existed,
So, to become even more mysterious, she had to be kissed.
Nevertheless, when I asked her later
to show me the direction to the nearest village,
she sent me the wrong way...

Really: presence is not just the present time!

The Snow

The snow started falling at midnight. And it is indeed true
that the best place to sit is in the kitchen,
even though it is a kitchen of sleeplessness.
It's warm there; you cook something for yourself;
you drink wine and look
from the window into an intimate eternity.
Why should you fret about whether birth and death are just points
when, after all, life is not a straight line?
Why should looking at a calendar agonize you?
Why should you worry about the name of the game?
And why should you admit that you don't
have enough money for Saskia's little shoes?
And why, then, should you boast
that you suffer more than others?

Even if there were no silence on earth,
that falling snow had already dreamed it up.
You are alone. Minimize your gestures.
There is nothing to admire.

A Test I

Hope in man, even the most enthusiastic one,
flung me, in the end,
under the might that was entirely human
and, thus, without God... Hence I have to exist,
and I am already punished,
especially because I may have led other souls astray...

Agonizingly, remorse after remorse
germinates in my heart.
The snake of irony vibrates its little tongue,
unequally equal in its bite.
However, suffering is precise.
If, at one time, evil brought me some joy,
today I am so horrified by such frequent killings
that they are already invisible!
If, at one time, habit brought me dread,
then I would willingly forego everything that I behold today,
so that, one day, freedom will have room
for what hope places there...

"Gilt your hand!" I told my despair,
"and drag music and wine here,
grasping their red hair, even if it means escape!"...
Leibniz, however, was mistaken... Even drunkenness
is not voluntary...
How then to live? How to live,
when already I can barely breathe,

while my death doesn't even think of
looking at the calendar?!...

It suffices to love it, and it will deceive itself...

Daybreak I

To Oldřich Králík

It is the hour
when the revolt of angels
holds faith without love.

It is the hour
when a scientist, who may have some emotion,
still does not believe.

It is the hour
when even a prayer for dead poets
falls flat, for they are already behind their reflections.

It is the hour
when everydayness is so mysterious
that it is already gone.

It is the hour
when you – though still alive – won't escape
through a secret entrance, nor under another name...

How?

How to live? How to be simple and verbatim?
I was always looking for a word
that was spoken only once,
even for a word that was, so far, not spoken at all.
I should have looked for words that are common.

Nothing can be mixed into wine,
even if the wine is not consecrated...

Yet Again

Although not even my friend understood my verses
(just as there are beings who can't kill,
even if they wanted to),
and although I was already desperate, completely
	abandoned
(just as there are some statues that were so horrified
by human sins that they turned into wood),
and although nothing else but suicide suggested itself to
	me,
I always felt this: to become nothing,
but to destroy even that nothing!

I already loved again...

What Might She Be Reading?

What might she be reading – that girl on the tram with a book?
Having been outside time and appearance,
and even outside a name,
she had nothing more but her heart,
which trembled with such devoutness
that, if she was to speak, she would be reviling,
and, if she was to glance up, she would catch sight of nothing
but a revolt and the fall of angels...

Those who descend into poesy
won't step up any more...

When It Rains on Sunday

When it rains on Sunday, and you are alone – absolutely
    alone,
being open to everything, when not even a thief is coming,
and neither a drunkard nor an enemy knocks at the door.
When it rains on Sunday, and you feel abandoned,
and you don't comprehend how to live without your body
and how not to be when you have a body.
When it rains on Sunday and you are entirely by yourself,
don't expect even a conversation with yourself!
Then only an angel exists, who knows just what's above
    him.
Then only a devil exists, who knows just what's under him!

A book in possession – a poem in desertion....

A Dying Poet

A hand with nails, coloured with my blood,
holds in its palm the stone of *your* heart.

For whom is that gift, when it is not a remedial bezoar?
And to whom belongs that heavy, feather-light hand?

I only surmise... I always used to have a presentiment,
and my thought was only an image,
and my heart was only a parable...
Indeed, a stream was also there,
but still without a surface... I protected freedom
for the price of life; I used to yearn and be astonished,
and, even if I might have had a vision without revelation,
I was so faithful that I became a witness...

The Noonday Witch

"The birch in the woods lashes the brushwood and stifles
 weeds,"
said the gamekeeper.
"In the water, it's the same!
There the perch is also a weedy fish,"
said the fish-master.

It was good that, not long after, the noonday witch walked
 by!
Both men hushed up and everything could love again:
all the trees and all the fish
out of ancient familiarity...

After St Martin's I

It was just before dawn when the first snow fell. Chaste and young,
as only a promise and a referral can be,
and only an apparition that agrees with perishable beauty...
Yet, well before the mortals,
who were watching its presence,
admitted – even if just with eyes half open –
their intoxicating languor and craving agony:
the earth made haste with its thirst, and the snow began to melt...
Yet, before it happened,
you ascertained, from a few footprints,
that someone walks and someone else just treads...

Any Night, Especially The One Before Dawn

So many people cannot sleep!
So many of them are hurrying away from themselves,
like a horse passing by a slaughter-house!
And so many of them tremble from their fright!
The full tread of all bones urges an escape with a swish.
Hissing lust abandons a leaking soul,
and even remorse flees into the never-to-be-seen.

Yes! The mirrors are exactly there...

There Are

There are things that are hidden from themselves.
Thus, almost human already,
they could reveal themselves within us
and, smilingly, open us up to everything.
However, our unconsciousness is more and more rare.
You know, it is warmer near beasts...

She

To arrive means a lot, but to wait means even more.
And she knows how to wait. For her,
graves are nothing more than nettle blisters
on the back of the self-tortured earth...
Although a simple chunk of earth is dearest to her,
and she almost hates monuments and daisies,
she enjoys hiding behind the trunks of shoddy trees.
Then later (even if she was to dish up only wax-fruit),
she welcomes, already in the garden, those
whom she invited into her home...

Without a Title I

Evil must do. Even that which need not be done,
despite the heart always trampling it down...
What to do, then, with a narrower gradation of blood
casting the shadow of Fate upon coincidence?
What to do with a half man on the body of a half-god?

Yes?

Even the one who might have died in love
at the resurrection of Christ the Lord
would not make it easier for his mother —
not even by one half-breath... Suffering walks with life
like the arts against Nature...
What a rose once laid bare
would be buried by the nose of a dead man...

And recollections are here only for the reason
that Time was decried...

Each of Them

Even a sinful priest is a priest...
However, a poet is supposed
to die when young and not to learn
even about the first kiss
and to be, in fact, thrown out and trampled by
      nightingales...

Who knows? It is night, and the wind, fused with rain,
pursues and wets two grey beards
somewhere on the cart road.
What if, in the end, each of them met
a blind horse?!

Grief

They say that grief is mute...
And yet the majority – even of those reserved ones –
long to open their hearts, to unburden themselves, to
    whine.
You were giving ear to them and suffered with them,
but you were always supposed to revere mystery:
you waited for inspiration,
which is usually precise, but never letter-perfect...

Being faithful, you could not be personal...
No doubt you never disclosed
the feelings of those who kept silent about them...

The Pedal Curve of a Parabola

You may be the first groom in the stables of Pegasus
and later the one who already boosted his being
by the fall of Lyrids up to sheer greatness –:

how hard it is now for you to find out about your essence,
though everything reasons with you
just to return, perhaps to rail-station sparrows,
and to feel, at last, your deplorable face:
the face with its mask in your hand alone!

She – Even the Sun Sometimes Replicates Itself and Points to Where It Is Not

To Libuše Widermann

She, always she, always present all the time!
However, even a horse – having been fed with barley
that was discovered in the bricks of pyramids –
is on the skyline, always the same,
but always without a rider...

I see all of her, receding towards the verdure in a tragedy,
while a wilted branch scrapes itself behind the ear of the
    wind,
and while some water bird
mocks her tears...

Autumn in Všenory

Fog... The forest heats with green branches...
A bird sits as a model to its own silence...
Not being edged, an unravelled leaf in a zero position
forebodes a word so heavy that an untenable book
would have to carry it away...

Even the longest poem in the world
lingers about its title and misses its end.
However, the one who has already started it
and does not know how to go on
should return to the first verse.

When Observing the Sun Spot at a Hornbeam

How inconspicuous it is at this trunk,
and how unwillingly it humbles that moment
when Pythagoras, in his love for boys,
stood at the foot of a theatre
and revealed his golden thigh!

How modest it is and how oblivious of
setting its foot into a name,
into the name of donors, or, as one would say: of witnesses,
even if it should not happen thus!

How kind it is, cherishing and *for* life in life,
where, otherwise, everything is so uncertain
that even a votive prayer still pleads...

Beauty Without Joy

Our mortality is ceaseless. There is no moment
that could refute for us
that we are in temptation all the time,
and that we always succumb to it,
so that even beauty makes no sense
because it is beauty without joy...
We are wicked... Would we be so wicked,
if we were without any witnesses?

The Distant One...

For the heart of loving women, the distant one
is space and thus has something of stars and trees – of
    rivers.
However, it suffices that a bat flies past them,
and they quickly cover up their crotches with their hands...

Being real, they are frightened of reality: "Are you really
    back?"
And knowing well man's sensitivity that can feed a stone,
they chase their fears away, as long as they can,
even if later, while fleeing, they should
secretly cross their own borders
with diamonds, sewn into the pockets of their vulva...

Verses

It is the time when they serve cabbage with anger
and a calf with hate;
it is the time when Death has thorn wine on tap;
it is the time when, the blinder it is,
the more goggle-eyed it becomes;
it is the time when field edges are ploughed up;
it is the time when even an ardent tear knows
that it cries alone;
it is the time when the wolf takes away whatever's been
 read;
it is the time when only souls are illuminated;
it is the time when it is *impossible* to love one's own
 misfortune
because it belongs to all your fellow creatures...

A Resort

Some time ago, it was a bath-house... Today, not even the
    wind loiters about,
and also those leached jackdaws hardly remember
the tennis shorts, scalded to their last thread,
and the pitfalls of female garters...
And, of course, not even evil spirits are there
because they were already banished long ago to waterless
    places;
they would only batten down dampness and mildew here,
where there is no difference between the roof and the
    floor...

Only walls, standing tightly together like a gunshot
and collapsing half-way down to their waists,
uncloak a hunchback in the inn yard there,
who, attired in clothes left by the dead Strauss,
chopped down all trees and all bushes
to ensure that, in the autumn, he doesn't have to sweep up
fallen leaves...

All the Time

A fateful year... It rained so much that it seemed
it would never rain again...
And such a swelter came that it appeared
it would never rain again...
It also seemed that such a year
was only once in a century, but it goes on,
and someone too is always giving back
love to passion, light to fire
for the price of a ravaged soul...

Daybreak II

The song of roosters... Daybreak opens an open door...
Melancholy, that never left, appears in them,
giving one of its hands to passion
and the other one to suffering.

And you believed that you were forgotten!

A Stopover of a Courier
To Václav Černý

If there were snow, a footprint would remain after me,
here, where, for a while, I lean on the wall of a hemp kiln...
However, all feels warm and greenish;
even women have made up their faces with malachite.
Rye already turns yellow, clouds grow heavy
and the pond mirrors them like morphine under one's
    skin...

The papyrus from Oxyrhynchus* is, in fact, too young
in comparison with what I am carrying... Is a war coming
    again...?

How silently a horse drinks...

---

* The Oxyrhynchus papyri are a group of manuscripts discovered at an ancient rubbish dump near Oxyrhynchus in Egypt, dated from the first to the sixth century AD.

The Sun at Candlemas

A snow storm... The sun, somewhere in Thuringia...
Otherwise there is nothing that would even resemble
    itself...
Dreams, signs, pictures, even the dampness of walls
could be saved only with supernatural help...

I loved and therefore I don't remember.
In life for life, death was coming to me,
but never to the same place;
even ignorance does not mean happiness...

My loneliness is horrid, as it dumbly commands me
not to be impersonal for whomsoever... A poem is a gift...
Yes, but what's spoken is better than what's written...
I would give anything for a friend!

At Insomnia

At insomnia, a brief slumber...
And then awakening, thrown out
into the chilly shoes of consciousness...
You feel as if it is raining,
and you are to get off your train in Chuchle,
while those from as far as Beroun are convinced
that they will live to see the sunrise before they arrive...

Your own shadow freezes you... Everything seems stupid,
like a poem written on a typewriter
or like a heated church...

Those Others

A cemetery chapel, seen over a garden wall,
where a cat devours a nightingale –
such was my vision of life.
I lived through it and don't know why I should offer
any apologies to whomsoever of the mortals.

Even the most unreserved declaration of love
is like a downfall of all living beings at once.
Even the most voiceless declaration of love
is like a resurrection of all graves at once.

Those others are coming to me, those others...

Let the Dead Bury the Dead

If those alive had their truth ahead of the dead,
it would be the end of both present and future remorse...

If those alive had their truth over the dead,
we who are alive would levitate...

However, it is just so:
Remorse yes – wings no!

To Whom?

He felt so parched,
as if even the fountain wouldn't put up with water,
the weir with the river, the bottle with wine...
Even when telling himself
that the present time follows itself too fast
so that it won't be the future any more,
he felt that man was, in fact, making a detour in both,
if he didn't suffer almost senselessly...

If he suffers so much, how is it that he does not bewail
    alone,
like bells sometimes start to clang by themselves?

But, isn't he doing just that?...

A Judgement

Not long ago, your engraved view of life
seemed to be certain. Why is it
that, not tired though not rested,
it is suddenly humiliated by the ambiguity of appearances?

In Rome, however, the stairs
up which Christ climbed to appear before Pilate
still remain...

After the Death of My Sister Rose

You died and my remorse – heaps of telegrams
from the least anticipated places –
changed my conscience into a promontory.
Its height is substantial and is, perhaps, already fixed,
while I am falling still lower and lower
and perhaps, but not until you have forgiven me
    everything,
I may burst into tears, as there are rivers with one spring,
and others with more...

The Adder Hunter

"Do you recall?" said the adder hunter to me.
"Suddenly – still before evening – there appears,
among clouds, the first *cumulus* of the year.
Although still half in captivity of its winter cold,
it is already autocratic... Look, it's March!

However, if it's true that the garments
of our first parents, when committing their first sin in
    Paradise,
were stripped from the skin of the snake who seduced Eve,
then, because of the warmth, I am still in winter,
and because of the chill, I am already in summer,
somewhere near the stumps, upon the rocks, in the sand
or near women..."

Is this Enough?

No, I can't go against the mask with an anti-mask!
Neither can I reverse!
I'd rather not allow my vision to find its voice.
I'd rather let everything that passion loses
be donated by melancholy
in its returning despair!

Wasn't this always
the only manifestation by the deed I knew?...
What more can anybody want from me?
Even laurel smells sweet only after it has faded.

Dies Caniculares 1951

July, impudently sprawled out between clouds
like a dog in bed –
and below: a hill, looking sideways at a squint-eyed desert,
and below: you, so tormented by your debts that you are
    even
afraid to cut the uncut pages of a book you've just bought...

Constricted breath and sultry heat only indicate
Death, standing at the river's entry into a lake –
and yet, it is unavoidable!

All right! I always used to ride out alone
but put saddles on two horses:
the second one for my double.
And, because they took off both our shoes,
we'll do it today with spurs on bare feet!

Recollection II

To František Tichý

When, for so many hours of criss-crossing,
we were looking in vain for some pimpernel,
we came out of the groves
and stopped, at the stroke of noon, in the moors.
The air was fried on a hot plate. We were looking
at the opposite hillside, thickly overgrown
with various bushes and trees. They were as numb as we were.
At that moment, I was just about to query something
when, in that immobile, shuddering,
spell-bound mass, a single tree,
in just one single place,
suddenly began to shiver
like a hexatonic tone but without sound.
You would have said that it was exultation from lightness
    of heart,
and, thus, almost an adventure in itself.
Then the tree started to rustle,
as silver rustles when it turns black.
Then the tree started to tremble,
as the skirt of a woman trembles when touching
the clothes of a man, while reading a book in a madhouse.
Then the tree started to shake and flounce,
as if it were shaken and flounced by someone
who peers into the black-eyed bottom of love –
and I felt as if I was just about to die...

"Don't be afraid," said my father, "it is an aspen!"
But I remember, to this very day, how he turned pale,
when we came there later
and saw an empty chair under it...

Non Cum Platone

Her beauty is destroying my love because,
through the destruction of illusion, it also destroys truth.

His love is destroying my beauty
because, after receiving a mask, I also want a curtain.

A bleak dawn... A hamlet,
where all roosters have been eaten...

The Eyes of a Man

What his eyes are, a man learns only from women,
and they don't have to be only those
who look into a mirror in the dark,
and not just at the moment when the clock
stops and a wooden fire dies out
and the trees copulate in an advent wind.

You learned about this from a gypsy woman,
who was sitting with a mug of cold coffee,
while one could hear a thrasher from behind the village
    backyards,
and then you understood
that chastity or artfulness
are terms that are indirect...

The second time, it was during a night brawl in Gahatagat.
You have no idea whether she was espoused to someone
    else,
but her eyes told you something in such a way
that it seemed as if you were both in an irrevocable time
and had therefore lost your childhood.

Then, with the feelings of a jealous murderer,
you understood
what a kiss – only a borrowed one, not a given one – was...

Only Over the Wall of a Boneyard

This hermitage, where man used to cut his hair crosswise,
to oust his sinful thoughts;
this hermitage, a womb, not fed,
unless with a cord around the loins;
this hermitage, a throat, waiting
for a ritual knife, used for cutting off one's breath;
this hermitage, where an angel is carved into sandstone
onto a rooster and the rooster onto a skull;
this hermitage, completely apart from itself, corresponds
to a poet's fame only over the wall of a boneyard...

Autumn II

Nightfall in the country in autumn;
a nightfall just for friendship...
Yet, in that countryside, a couple appear,
evidently asking their way
because a farmer points with his whip.
"I love you because –" says the man
to a woman of bad reputation.
"I remember," says the woman to the man,
"how, at home, they always claimed that the one
who slept under a yew-tree would die...
We shall walk on, shan't we?"

Wild geese are close to taking off.
Chilliness purifies the river.
The water spirit goes to warm himself up in a grower's
    hut...

After St Martin's II

It was some time after St Martin's...
At that time, I walked across the plane
of Gahatagat... I felt
as if I didn't know what date it was...
But snow had been falling for a long time...
Everything was snowbound...
And, at one moment, the wind blew so hard
that I bowed my face down
and suddenly noticed – with my shortened soul –
that, always one step ahead of me, there was a fresh
    footstep...
No living soul was around me...
Who, then, could walk in front of me?
It was I who walked in front of me...

In Temptation

One hour from midnight... The rooster sings...
It helps me so much and scares my nightmares,
since this third candle in front of me
is, anyway, only a repetition of the two that burned out;
they burned out with a downturn of radiance
and in such a dive
that it could land only in Hell.

Then Satan could easily metamorphose
into an angel of light, take wing and be here...
O rooster, sing, sing! I like you!

Mountains Go, Flowers Go

The crows turn their beaks towards mountains...
Spring is coming...
We too, from time immemorial, only demand...
Time marches from what's empty into what's desolate
and stands alone...
The pulse of my heart is irregular. How then
can the rhythm of my verses be the same?

Ardently abandoned into the will of poesy!

Under the Hill of Blaník

A poet cannot hope in man alone.
Neither is he Elias,
to have a raven bring him bread.
The road to *gallantry* is tedious;
such a road requires patience,
just as fire is made at the place
where an incendiary started it...

Not even the weather is always chasing rainbows;
the weather is like a pub, where an angel in a mackintosh
sits quietly at a table
and refuses some quick soup –
a sort of watered-down one –
and waits for a bottle of wine
already redeemed a long time ago,
and thus exonerating...

A poet is *perhaps* an originator,
if he was accorded with that blessing,
but never a creator. How then would he
be accepted by Plato
into an ideal community
if he refuses self-adoration?

Near the River Jizera

To Jaroslav Durych

How beautiful is that domelike flint wall
against the ice! The river below
also admires it, as I do, in an old-fashioned way.
The river is beside itself and, when she does not know how
and with what she should compare it, she simply mirrors it.
Compared with these boulders, not desecrated by man,
how cruel was the fate of gravestones and altar tablets...

Today, of course, they quarry stone only for dungeons...

31.1.1952

An October Day

This morning, our neighbour cuts the throat of a rooster;
it had been attacking women.
Its blood drops onto the newspaper, beside which
an inconspicuous knife lies... From the corner of a grove,
the wind scatters cinders at the grate of a sweet briar
    bush...
At the river sills, virgins spread out their sanitary napkins...
A swash of wine between Death's eyes...
But we won't be in excess...

Then it starts raining... The rain in the orchard
colours its hair with elderberries...

During a Night

That beautiful Morello cherry alley,
through which a farmer now strides
with one and a half score of crayfish in his bag,
is illuminated for him
by the nocturnal pollution of the Milky Way
and by a pecuniary radiance...

At the same time, someone else walks
along a deserted, hollowed-out farm track,
and, although the moon is past its third quarter,
he soon finds himself under a knoll and tells himself:
"Hardly anywhere now
shall we see Calvary with three crosses.
It is usually only one cross with Christ the Lord,
because anyone of us can substitute
those two malefactors on each side of Him..."

Ubi Nullus Ordo, Sed Perpetuus Horror

It is frightful to live because one has *to remain*
in the appalling reality of these years...
Only a self-murderer thinks that he can leave through a
    door
that is merely painted on the wall...
There is not the slightest sign of Paraklet's coming...

The heart of poesy pains me...

At Marat's Grave

Like a heavy sleep, the one who is heavy
is not deep.

The knife of Charlotte Corday
immediately hits the floor.

Also, it is surely in the shallows that he lies here,
under this colossal maple tree;
a colossal one, because trees
planted above a dead dog flourish.

An Old Priest

To Josef Vašica

We met each other at Charles' Bridge; it snowed.
I have not seen him for almost twenty years.
Have I complained? I might have,
because he tried to cheer me up,
and, when I was talking about sin, he said gently:
"Yes, after all, how could we recognize you
at the Last Judgement?!"
However, when this didn't help, he said suddenly:
"My son, it seems to me that you now despise abstractions
in your verses... Your desire for austerity
would be commendable, if it were subtle...
However, you act as if, with one part of your spirit –
namely the most adventurous one –
you don't want to be under God's authority.
Don't you enjoy drinking wine?"

Down to the Last Cent

They looked him in the eye, so as not to see into his eyes;
they looked at the world as if at something unheard of;
they were running from Annas to Caiaphas
and from Caiaphas to Pilate,
while they followed him scornfully,
thinking: Besides being God's gift, damn him!

But he was alone,
as if he didn't belong to this generation;
he was alone, because love had descended into his heart
and he became too large;
he was alone, with a question obstinately imposed,
like the last day before the house-rent collection quarter;
he was alone, like a sleeping man...

But to be alone, even in one's wakefulness?
Yes, after all, even the soul's centre
is permanently ahead of pain...

Spices of the Holy Ghost

For someone – through a sidetrack,
for someone else – forthrightness...

For someone – both grief and joy,
for someone else – only woes...

Pocket your pride; don't repine; don't ask why;
it can't be any other way;
you shall be a poet, even after your death.

You Found...

In old prayer books, you found a fragment
of the following love letter: "– also,
you should be as simple
as the shadow of the Guardian Angel
or a farmer in the moonlight.
But you: every one of them altogether and each one
    separately,
and that's illicit... From someone like that
one would rather run away with Paris
onto a black ship... If you can, fill in what's missing,
just you alone now, though I doubt
that you know how to do it,
but just to tell God is to do it...

And that little scar of mine left by immunisation
that you have ... then ... in the hall..."

A Watchman's Song

Burns was right... But I am convinced
that it is impossible to *visualize* any woman
from reading books, let alone from reality.
She *exists*. And it is only thanks to her
that men also exist, more often as murderers,
who, like kings, sometimes share
the crown diamonds of her mystery...

The Asphalt Princess

Forever and a day, that woman there won't stop
shuffling her feet to warm herself up...

The Eddington Star also shuffles its feet,
though only until it has found its equilibrium...

The former lowers her hat so that one can't see into her
 eyes,
the latter looks so that one can't see into its eyes...

Home

You agonize about who should be awarded the victory:
whether the material or ethereal state of the soul,
and then, you feel how much alone you are,
separated from your dear ones by the mute side of the
    door...

It takes many nights until, one morning,
when your daughter, not yet three years old,
already reaches the door handle and opens it...

How it warms, how it warms! After all,
an angel indeed signifies a message...

They Have...

They have their memories, which I don't have;
I remember, and they cannot remember with me,
but, in the end, it is always the same: it concerns the dead...

All that amidst sighs in pitiless silence,
as if a calcant player pedalled the bellows,
and there was nobody at the organ...

Without a Title II

One says that Druids' boulders move.
Yet women's beauty, just by their steps, is much more cruel.
A heart-broken poet writes it down in this world:
a world that sometimes hears, only grudgingly,
about remoteness and adventure,
and, cynically, it decries and belittles even wonderment...

A proud spirit cannot be a tragic spirit.

A Fall

In every book there is a place with a woman
whom we would want to kiss so much
that she would have a moon eclipse in each corner of her
 eyes,
and we would feel as if she were
blindfolding us before our execution...

In every book there is such a place
where we love sin. It is not always an unhappy love.
Oh yes, I know that even blood gives smoke...
The sex of a book... But dreams can't be interpreted...

A Test II

To Radovan Lukavsky

We can see it daily: soldiers let their horses drink
from the coffins of saints... It is true that Nature
seems not to care... Just at this moment,
an owl flies out and an eagle-owl slips in,
and the black thorn blossom still follows instructions from
 the stars,
and there are still children and mothers, and also a
 drunkard,
who was late for Holy Mass,
and there is still much more: for example pain
and heath's scent under the gravity of the penultimate
 wasp...

And there is still much more, and there's already too little
 of it,
before this world will be destroyed, before it destroys itself,
for Maxwell's demon has already matured into a devil,
and science may soon construct a model of God...

The Body of a Woman

All my words, destroyed by naked wonder,
talk about the body of a woman... Aware of its beauty,
it challenges my muteness
for languor, for song, for adoration, even for augury,
but, as if something missing should still be added,
lust is already here...

Every love is star-crossed...

You Know It, My God!

You know it, my God: like joy, sorrow too can
    communicate.
Even the one who's been completely abandoned
by people, by phantoms, by beasts and by things,
and who then communicates alone with himself,
does not say it for his own sake!...

The Fourth Month

An April fog. The one and only sunray,
as blind as the walking stick of a blind man,
gropes its way, albeit more firmly than a week ago.
Cold hands – an ardent heart...

You, too, and more than you anticipate... But that's all...
If some danger threatens you, you are defenceless...
If some stroke of happiness threatens you, you are
    powerless...

† To My Sister Rose

You, who return from the world beyond,
be mindful, oh, be mindful of those
who froze to death along their way, and of me,
the only one who survived from the whole platoon
that was accompanying me. I alone deliver myself
into the deportation blockhouse of remorse,
knowing that everything is punishment...
A punishment for life!

What Then?

I never rode on horseback,
and also I never changed from a horse to a donkey;
I was always on foot... And yet you say:
Be direct!

To be direct!... Yes! But the word
does not want to move away from the search for its spirit,
which is surely omnipresent;
the word does not want to move, does not want to move
unless forced by madness...

December in a Village

A dawn that gives too little light; a dawn
that a farmer would compare with a cow before calving...
Soon, of course, it is compensated by snow,
which keeps lying around so permanently
that it is, in fact, bronze that witnesses impermanence...

But there is already someone who rakes up some fabric
from the wardrobe, the fabric whose colour
both the next spring sun and someone
who recognizes the voices of all birds will pull out...

Resurrection

To Stanislav Zedníček

After this life here, should it be a terrifying clamour
of trumpets and bugles that would awake us one day?
Forgive me, God, but I console myself
that the beginning and the resurrection of all of us, the
    deceased ones,
will simply be announced by a rooster's crow...

We then stay lying down for a while...
The first person who gets up
will be mother... We'll hear her
quietly kindling the fire,
quietly putting the kettle on the stove
and placidly taking out the coffee-grinder from the
    cupboard.
We'll be home again.

A Voice

"I do not understand your complaints
about being bitterly alone.
Suffer with those who suffer, and you won't be one of them!
But if you are so bitterly alone,
hold on, and they will find you!"

Deep in the Night

Who woke you up inside such a bewitching silence?
And why is it
that you suddenly see the chapel – some few miles distant –
in which you were once baptized,
and, in that chapel, a ballad with a knife in its hand,
which stopped in front of a sweating tombstone?

The mystery, handed down by your ancestors,
makes your spine shudder...

October I

With what harmonious sympathy
(his head tilted by the vicinity of heart murmurs)
a thrush watched a falling birch leaf today!
And, at the same time, how forgivingly
the neighbours talked at the backyard door
about where and to which graveyard
they would let themselves be buried after they died!

What, then, could these things mean to you:
some fragments of Phaedrus* from Oxyrhynchus;
Newton commenting on the Apocalypse;
Philip II commenting on Erasmus,
or an alpine waterfall, flown through the kidneys of
    Byronism!

---

* Phaedrus – a dialogue between Plato and Socrates about love, composed around 370 BC

Premonition

To Bohumil Rejsek

A lovely morning... with enough fog to make fifty chemises
for the *Lady of the Lake*... Later, a moment
when a warm August tastes of wine...
Horror from a collar made of coffin shavings...
A bright desire for life...

However, if your heart is ill,
you will seek its health in the Underworld
but won't return any more...

Poesy

She said: No, not today, some other time,
only some other time, later, later!

He said: Yes, you are postponing,
while you should be preceding a poet.
After all, even the clothes left by Shakespeare
were from Hamlet's wardrobe...

But Love Both...

The disparity of earth and thus the disparity of men
can be felt only if you kneel down.
But love both of them and, indeed, so much more,
because there are no loves, because there is only one love,
just as all crosses are only one cross.

A Pine

How beautiful is that old Weymouth pine
at the hill of your youth,
which you visited again today...
Under its murmur, you remember your dead
and ponder upon the arrival of your turn.
Under its murmur you feel
as if you have just finished your last book
and now are supposed to keep silent and cry,
so that the word can grow...

What was your life? You deserted your friends for
    strangers.
And your fate? It smiled at you only once,
and you were not there...

In a Cloud

Aridity, hopelessness, lassitude, lethargy...
Not having two pennies to rub together...
Why then keep asking
about the sense of human life,
and whether or not we've been here long enough?

A dew drop, a woman, a warbler
mocking other birds;
friendship, jealousy (which was once
dancing the whole night under the moonshine
until even its shoes turned silvery);
love, music, a book:
no, it tells you nothing more...

Without a Title III

To Julius Bartošek

Disjoined consciousness has blocked your way
to eternal life by freedom without God.
Now everything for you is only an appearance, not a
   revelation;
a phantom, not a vision;
a phrase, not a pronouncement; a generality...
Gone are the major voices of the heart,
seeking harmony that madness could not nourish...

A Test III

A circular eclipse... Thus, Eros as a planet...
But melancholy contains,
as a condition, something of eternity
that would be arrested in madness...

Later then, it seems that pain
could exist even in heaven...

A Chicken

The door opens by itself
in front of an angel... Another time, it is a chicken,
which comes from the backyard as far as the kitchen.
It is so capriciously looking at those who are there
that none of them waits for what happens next
and each quickly crosses himself with a defensive gesture...

A Night

Not even Homer felt so miserable
in front of Helen for being in love with her,
because he didn't fall in love for love,
but for beauty. No, not even Homer
felt so miserable in front of Helen
as you, who fell in love with the one
who brings the shrouds of those still alive
to the moon's mangle...

Quite Certainly

A priest invokes the name of God –
we provoke it.
This has been taking place for centuries,
and our century decided in a frenzy
to perpetuate it until pride was immortalized.

But quite certainly someone has already been chosen
to polish the armour of Archangel Michael...

Death

Yet again, it goes around like dripping wet air
on an incendiary's skin,
or like the environs of a brewery when it malts...
I see it clearly in the gash, in that incision
by the black diamond of Adam
into the glass of virginity...

In the Nothingness

In the nothingness, as fatty as a thick book
discoursing upon a lost lyrical poem
of an unknown poet –
we who sweat instead of shedding tears,
we who say that a crying stone sweats,
thought today of the one who drowned
while learning to swim in order not to drown...

Meantime, the park behind the window – once so refined –
muzzled the wind's sleeve with verdure's nose
and then studied the mistletoe with its eyes...

On a Biting Night

Once at night, I heard
a walnut tree burst by frost.
It banged like shrapnel
at the conquest of Babylon –
shrapnel that would not explode until now...

The landlord ran out of his manor, a horse from the stable,
and I had the idea to open
my white book for the summons to consciousness...

We don't even surmise,
and then we become astonished...

I Don't Understand

A poet and an exaggeration say...
as if an intuitive life
could not be an active life!
I don't understand! What do they mean by that?
That an act gives witness,
but a gift is to be a compliment?
For example, once in Greece,
I became aware of my *mortality*
only because I had a strong desire for a god's wife...
I lost it in drinking bouts with Marlow...

El Todo

To Rudolf Havel

Nothingness, all alone within itself
but without confidence in itself,
sates its lust:
the visible one upon life, the unseen one upon existence...

The deepest place of the soul: nadir,
called cunningly back...

Once

Once a guest, then a foreigner and in the end an impatient
    phantom,
I always used to yearn for certainty
that at least those whom I love are really alive.
Although my love might have been as wild as it was,
I only touched them with my wounds...
O remorse, you are so ancient that you are as fresh
as once, when, under some eloquent hill,
I inhaled some minute foliage of wormwood
at the highest status of gentian,
while the moon spun the wall of China inside an imperial
    head!

The Blinded Ones

The admiring, marvelling light, similar to the one
under which Pontius Pilate asked for a portrayal
of Christ the Lord...

Not the tiniest cloud, not the merest nightfall,
so much desirable to us
for whom only darkness reveals a good deal...

Inside You

Without any excuse and thus ineloquent
is this:
it is not possible to observe one's own sins
as Galileo could do with sunspots.
Also, the road to Damascus
is inside you...

Seen from an Express Train

Seen from an express train, which takes a shadow as truth...
Even so, she was veritably beautiful,
and she was bareheaded;
she was bareheaded, as if an angel
forgot his head here
and went off with her little hat...

A Test IV

Sleeplessness, qualms of conscience, dread,
whizzing through a house without windows and doors
as far as my heart: there, where all hope ends...

But above, the enormous radiance of night,
overfilled with itself,
enters the shadow of the smallest star...

God creates – a poem springs up.

Children

To Jiří Brdlík

There are children... In fact, only they...
Purity of heart, self-evidence of a miracle
of which we adults are denied, even if astonished
like a little fire that broke off from the heart of poesy...

There are children – in fact, only they!
I do not know why they tear their books and marionettes,
but only children are eternal,
like a lark's song over the battle at Austerlitz...

In Between

In between an idea and a word,
there is more than we are able to comprehend.
There are ideas for which no words can be found.

A thought, lost in the eyes of a unicorn,
reappears in the laugh of a dog...

In September, Close to 2 am

At a snuffed out candle, you sometimes feel
that you have discerned. As if one said: he turned blind
there, where you should have seen...
You left all your young years there,
your bad trail in good soil,
and now you are obviously old and secretly sick...

But don't be afraid, you won't die yet:
Death is still in the orchard,
shaking a plum tree...

Mors Ascendit Per Fenetras

It may be that demons can pierce through walls;
it may be that Death really enters through windows,
but only Jesus Christ could enter through a closed door,
and then only to the Apostles...

Our one and only Guardian Angel comes not, leaves not;
he is with us all the time, faithful to us
and human in his compassion; he is with us all the time,
with me already for almost fifty years – and yet,
not until today, did it cross my mind, while drinking wine,
that I have never invited him
to have a drink with me...

Nothing Melancholy

There is nothing melancholy between earth and heaven
this morning. It's as if everything
had been living in the same beauty all those years.
How amazing, if one imagines
that man was created in God's image,
and so he *resembles* God!
Yet instead of wondering,
he goes blind from vertigo and jumps into that abyss...

Maliciously

All the time this horror is
cohabiting with its fluttered heart...
Something is in front of you,
similar to the derangement of a forest
with some light moments of darkness...
Yes, only a black boar sometimes has golden eyes...

Lovers

Time on the mountains: jealousy, the fruit of disbelief.
Time at a spring: infidelity, the fruit of jealousy.
Time at a river: jealousy without love.
Deaf, but at the top of carnality's voice...

Never Enough Tears

It was a long time ago: as if we were supposed to stream
against some toppled giants...

Later on, it was a Minoan jug,
created once and for ever,
when thirty gods drank from their bare palms
in front of a potter...

Today, Death keeps human tears in a thermos flask
to preserve their poignancy...

When It Is Foggy, Rust Falls upon Old and Beauty Falls upon Young Virgins

For the sake of beauty, or for the sake of love?
For the sake of beauty without joy,
or by virtue of love for the sake of beauty?
For the sake of love that is not love, but mere lovemaking?
And with grace, not yet given but already taken:
just for the sake of copulation?

An Oak Tree

O you century old tree! The main branches of yours
are dead... But with every spring,
you turn green with a tiny shoot.

O you ancient life! Graveyards have outgrown you
right up to death... And yet, again and again,
it is a child you lead by the hand!

The Year 1953

O hope! My mind is ailing.
I can't wait to see you; I walk along a platform,
but with such impatience that I ask only about express
    trains.

Only women know how to wait,
because they always come late to a rendezvous.
O hope! My mind is ailing!...

Partus Labyrinthis

Look, my lady, there are so many of my sins
that you can't find your way around them.
And there are so few of them
that you know them all.

Those that you know are all one sin –
and those you can't find your way around
are again the one
that confuses you, as much *as me*,
all the time!

Who?

From your beauty, who could recede?
Only your breast, that's yours, indeed.

Before your eyes, what can be read?
Only the book that diamonds set.

Who deafens here vanity's gush?
Only your laugh in laughter's rush.

Why do you fall like a lost leaf
and walk through trees for your relief?

Too much of you is no respite.
My day wants you, my sleepless night.

At Harvest Time

The sun poured out sugarless brandy,
recording it with moonmilk
upon the skin of reapers...

Without saying a word, haste began to talk,
with the swishing of scythes and machines.
On the horizon, with the grating of barns
rolled like a rural storm,
it had enough of itself to care about...

Then it was a horse
that stepped into a wasp's nest
and was stabbed to death.

Remembrance of September 1952

The itch of an autumnal wall,
scratched to the blood of a thicket creeper...
What a wonder that you, a Czech poet, don't beg...
But, to rely on man
is like not believing in God,
and still wanting a miracle...

At the End of June

No, it's not possible to sleep... The younger the silence now,
the more sonorous the particulars of grey remorse...
I pace my room at midnight,
sewing the nooks together into a pile of despair...
Who is spitting in my face?
Is the end of innocence inside a poet?
In the sky, Leo and Virgo are setting...

Why?

Once again, I was avidly spiteful!
I know that even the soul's finest blade
is willing to cut the roughest cloth into words.
But why am I doing this? After all, it is not
until love meets silence that I resound...

A Sunspot

A black sunspot, seen during the passage of Venus
across the sun... A winged vulva...

But down here: an act at the heels of a word...
But down here: everything's a sentence, a life-sentence...

A Dream

A dry depth from the ends of memory
frays out into the hairs that attained Hell.
A shamelessly insistent abstention. A laugh.
I never took men seriously,
says lady Macbeth,
contemplating her palms,
stained with blood from killing drunken mosquitoes...

La Belle Dame Sans Merci

She sat at the pile of wood and sang.
I felt as if I was hurting myself with tenderness.

I felt as if I was yearning without hope,
disdaining tears and yet pampering them.

I felt as if the sun was eavesdropping through clouds,
like a thrush with a cherry in its beak.

I felt as if the brook nearby, full of trout,
became suffused with that song.

I felt as if... But she stopped singing and said:
"Don't go there; it is cold there!"
And I said: "Where? I can't see it anyway!"

Autumn III

To Bohuslav Reynek

A field of four furrows... An edge... A meadow... A pond...
Fieldfares feasting on rowanberries...
A spider, again picking up a dropped stitch...

A lovely day, expelled from reason
into autumn's heart... The wind turned purple...
A mosquito pillar carries the bosom of a dance...

Dolour and languor, memories and remorse...
Would you wish to be young again?
Would you like to live through all that once more?
Out of near and nearby remote shadows, one can hear
the charnel house in the village being nailed with tin...

Blackness

Our decline results from tasting fullness.
In the middle of gaiety, blackness will blacken more.
But, around the throat of tragedy,
that blackness is lily-white, like Shakespeare's neckband.

During Illness

A melting icicle, a leaking water tap,
a chronology of medicine drops.

Tibet sees through water. We through our tears...

The Epoch

It is through imaginary things
that we are still inside Time.

But today, before the Sower stepped forth,
the Reaper is already here.

It seems
that no dead and no living being will remain...

A Virgin

The festivities are over! So many lights were there
that darkness was perfect.
And he was there. And she didn't mind that it was he,
the very one, who was already passionate from wine,
but whose thoughts were still in the grapes...
Towards morning, he left her. And, now, she looks –
through a little hole in her Sunday dress –
at a naked nail of Monday...

At Night

In the absence of a beloved wife,
darkness, like a complete fool, borrows her feet,
slides into her shoes of ice
and starts dancing away from your bed
into a huge hall of insomnia...

Shoes clang, whirl, trample, frolic
without mercy, openly, for ever.
And they certainly feel good – dancing with someone else!
Your love, without faith, only helps them
from jealousy into adultery.
You hear them the whole night – more and more frostily –
and they don't melt until
they return to you again...

At a Fountain with the Ruby Fairy

Every beautiful woman is cruel,
obscurely humbling those naked men
who desire to drink straight from bedrock.

Yet, it is Death who comes intimately close to them,
like a sparrow at a railway station,
when they are unwrapping bread at the platform...

I am going to have children, says Death.

To Rose

Your apple orchard – since you died –
has grown. Now, its branches are longer.
The more your phantom tries to hide,
the more all twigs are true and stronger.

They bend, those branches and green twigs;
it seems there'll be lots of apples.
But, without you, they are just things.
We'll follow soon, time hardly matters...

Sultry Heat I

Over-ripe millet leaks. Birds drain it out.
The air feels like a burning headache.
A hand at the cross-roads catches quivering air.
Death, too, has eyes larger than a stomach.
In the only shadow, which resembles
the upturned delta of a female crotch,
a viper is ready,
like a dynamite safety fuse
in the lime rocks near Beroun...

Dust

To František Tichý

Degas used to model even dust on the bodies of danseuses;
but what about those many books there, sunk in dust!
It's a comfort to see someone crying here and there.
It's a comfort to see drowned water raining
upon rivers and lakes!
Yes, but from the bottom that you can't reach
one can hear a catfish eating up the remains of Ophelia...

Not Before

From an evening nail to a morning claw,
it was not the demon that caused my fright.

Not even the angel frightened me,
while painting himself upon himself.

An antique god on a pinnacle of dung
did not raise my fears.

Wild beasts were quite near and lamblike.
Insects did not analyse my feelings.

Timid, I ran wild, but
not before I got to know man

An Autumn Night

A couple of trees, still green, are abreast with the acidity
of a park, defoliated long ago,
because the sharp scent of its whiskey
is already in the second still.

The finger alphabet of a deaf-mute is not as mad
as the moon, which shares so many sunrays
that one of them is enough for it.

Yet, somewhere behind an illicit tapestry,
someone has already drained a glass
without touching it with his lips.

Yet, somewhere behind a wall,
harmonious with the flight of woodlice,
a man lies, requiring what's due
from an absent woman...

October II

To the red-hot iron of a man,
a woman is not water...
It's unpleasant to behold one's own face...
It is better to rove through the woods
and, with three dead martens, redeem
a captured squirrel from the gamekeeper,
then set it free...
How quickly it disappears into the weighty pine grove,
while her last look says:
"If you wish, wait for me in about one year!"

On Spy Wednesday*

It is a two-handed sword with which
the Old Testament browses in the New...
The transoms of a bell tower squeak... The bell bursts...
The turmoil of the world resounds
to the four corners of stolen heavens.
The Holy Ghost has no place to sit down.

Only a dead man, who took a walk in his rightful shroud,
has annual rings of stone for his eyes...

* In Christianity, Holy Wednesday (also called Spy Wednesday) is the Wednesday of the Holy Week, the week before Easter.

Along the Way

In Memory of Josef Florian

Leaning against a tree, which is afraid of lightning,
you feel that there will be lots of apples this year.
A couple, Adam, just yesterday in a virgin,
laughs and, with a one year old branch, drives away
the flies from around bovine eyes.
In a nearby flourmill, a millstone runs.
The brook, fleetingly swollen by rain,
intimately presses upon you to stay...
It is really lovely here,
and lovely also is the visible shouting –
but why is it always children who love to climb
over a graveyard's wall?...

Towards Poesy

You don't know whence that road comes
that will take you nowhere.
Yet you care very little about it; after all, it was full of
    magic,
women, wonders and craving for freedom.
You imagined a horse killed under an angel;
the angel walked – that's the way of self-oblivion –
and only then you learned about the grief of man,
but of God, too, who also seeks happiness –
that disconsolately loving God...

Awoken...

Awoken by some tapping on the window,
I went to look who was there.
But it was only a night and a willow and a dried-out wall
and a pane of glass in front of my hands,
all having shown themselves silently and simply.

Later, however, when I wanted to lie down again,
I saw a slumberer in flapping blankets:
it was my madness.

Sultry Heat II

The sun burns like a woman from the left side of her dress.
A snake, its whole body like a stone, and, in the sand, a
 wryneck.
Black spots behind me, black spots in front of me.
A fountain stands. I have to kneel down.

Someone

Someone tells you in your dreams: A thousand years ago...
Nothing more than this: A thousand years ago...
You wake up in horror, and it is the present,
shaken up by jet planes into the future,
where again it will be Homer's *courage of flies*[*]
over the dead...

[*] One of Homer's brilliant metaphors: flies, which, though driven unceasingly from the milk pails, are sure to return again.

Adonis

To whom the head? The head to sleep.
To whom the hair? The hair to grass.
To whom the body? The body to nakedness...
This is the way he sleeps, and one can hear
his private parts sparkling, combed by the hairbrush of
    Venus,
and one can see the knot left by the branch
that her vulva cut off...

After a Storm

The heat-stroke tempted the storm for so long
that it conceived a son from it,
who had the pulse of his heart in the lightning,
his throat in the thunder and his voice in the downpour...

Then all turned silent...
Only half-shadows danced in the stillness,
and only the stillness smelled fiercely,
like the sweet flag that we threw
under the priest's feet at Corpus Christi.

They Paint

With a wet brush, lime and glue,
how pungent the voice of the decorator sounds,
who, with wax in his ears, talks to himself
like an orphan, but with such confidence
as if promises wound down to an agreement!

To what agreement? It leaves you with a chilly feeling...

In Fallow

That unstumpable piece of land
is as good as it is...
The earth, ploughed up with force,
deforms both the mind and the feelings of man.
Bloom, heath! Smell sweet, you, so alone with freedom!
It is good not to catch sight of a human being here;
it is good not to hear a horse coughing here!

Succinctly

Man: sometimes, but only sometimes.
Nature: always, but only always.

Time is still to be fulfilled...

On the Sixth of January

The day of candles, which lick
a fish bone left from Christmas Eve.
But what's very beautiful
is that wooden mortar for pounding poppy seeds
in the deep foreground of a straw wall,
and that antique silence is also beautiful,
and why should Time care about some weeks?
Appearances don't bluff.
And it's freezing, but, in spite of that,
the gravestone is still warm.
That's because it moves...

It Was Already Late

A dreary day of wrinkled things, zip-fastened into
 decadence
through an invisible abyss.
"And what is fatality in our will?" asked a guard,
who had antagonized Night.
"Why stay alive?" asked a self-murderer.
"Why live again?" asked someone who had just died.

It was already late, when a woman came and asked:
"Which one of you can say: If you are not born,
I myself will be born?"

You May Ask

A fulfilled wish, and joy despairs of it.
A dream, made pointless by an act.
An image running amok, until it is explained
that there is nothing equivalent in nature.
Empty space of comprehension...

Ask a tear about what is left to be annihilated.

A Sparrow

A sparrow, leaving a snow-covered twig,
set it swinging a little, so that it's saying *yes*
with the negation of blind sentimentality.

A little snow is falling from that twig.
In a short time, it will change into an avalanche.

Goodbye

Again a storm drags on, out of the gossamer nook of Fate.
Consciousness, overcome by weakness,
goes in fear of an inside-out carnality.
Who dances, wearing the coat of bats' wings?
Who turns silent by the rumble of what he perceives?
Water from a well lures a youth, but a man seeks a spring.
All that is gone. There are words
that must not be talked about.
Never more will you fulfil a given promise.
Your skull dreamed out your eyes.

But

A long time ago, the god of laughter and song
had already closed Eternity behind himself.
Since those times, it is only rarely
that a diminishing recollection resounds in us.
Since those times, it is only pain
that never comes life-sized
but is always greater than man.
And yet, it must fit into his heart...

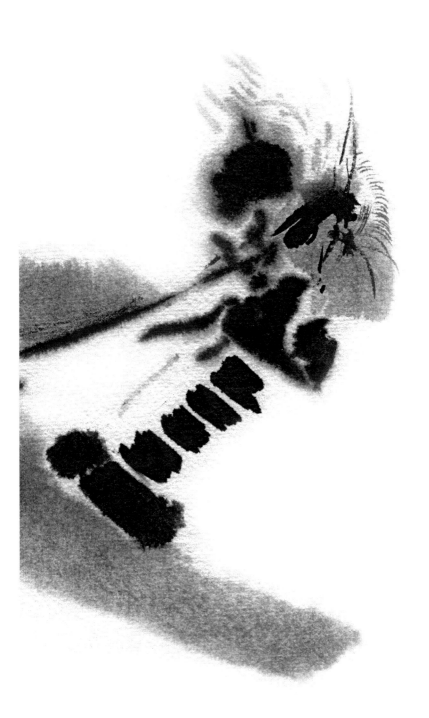

Translation: Josef Tomáš
Editing: Betty Boyd
Foreword: Jiří Brabec
Illustrations and graphic design: Jáchym Šerých
Typography: Mikoláš Fabián

Published 2010 by arima publishing

Lightning Source UK, Ltd.
Milton Keynes UK

Lightning Source UK Ltd.
Milton Keynes UK
UKOW030929150112

185439UK00001B/3/P